buddha mind

Also by Sangharakshita

A Survey of Buddhism
A Guide to the Buddhist Path
The Three Jewels
What is the Dharma?
Through Buddhist Eyes
Know Your Mind
The Taste of Freedom
Peace is a Fire
Human Enlightenment
The Religion of Art
The Eternal Legacy
Travel Letters
Alternative Traditions
Who is the Buddha?
Ambedkar and Buddhism
Crossing the Stream
The History of My Going for Refuge
Flame in Darkness
The Ten Pillars of Buddhism
Vision and Transformation
New Currents in Western Buddhism
The Rainbow Road *(memoirs)*
Facing Mount Kanchenjunga *(memoirs)*
In the Sign of the Golden Wheel *(memoirs)*
The Inconceivable Emancipation
Ritual and Devotion in Buddhism

The Buddha's Victory
Tibetan Buddhism: An Introduction
The Priceless Jewel
The Bodhisattva Ideal
The Call of the Forest and Other Poems
A Stream of Stars
The Drama of Cosmic Enlightenment
The FWBO and 'Protestant Buddhism'
Wisdom Beyond Words
Forty-Three Years Ago
The Meaning of Conversion in Buddhism
Complete Poems 1941–1994
Was the Buddha a Bhikkhu?
In the Realm of the Lotus
Transforming Self and World
Buddhism for Today – and Tomorrow
The Essence of Zen
What is the Sangha?

Booklets
Buddhism and the West
Great Buddhists of the Twentieth Century
The Meaning of Orthodoxy in Buddhism
Extending the Hand of Fellowship
My Relation to the Order
Going for Refuge

Sangharakshita

buddha mind

WINDHORSE PUBLICATIONS

Published by
Windhorse Publications
11 Park Road
Birmingham, B13 8AB
e-mail: windhorse@compuserve.com
web: www.windhorsepublications.com

Printed by
Interprint Ltd
Marsa, Malta

Cover design Karmabandhu
Cover photo Sakyamuni Buddha, mid-11th–12th century, western Tibet,
© John Bigelow Taylor; background photo: Photodisc

British Library Cataloguing in Publication Data:
A catalogue record for this book is available
from the British Library
ISBN 1 899579 43 5

Breaking Through into Buddhahood was originally published in *Mitrata no.10,
1976. Mind – Reactive and Creative*, was originally published in *The Middle Way*
(August 1971), and is reproduced by kind permission of the editor.

Contents

About the Author

Sangharakshita was born Dennis Lingwood in South London, in 1925. Largely self-educated, he developed an interest in the cultures and philosophies of the East, and realized that he was a Buddhist. The Second World War took him to India, where he stayed on to become the Buddhist monk Sangharakshita. After studying for some years under leading teachers from the major Buddhist traditions, he went on to teach and write extensively. He also played a key part in the revival of Buddhism in India, particularly through his work among followers of Dr B.R. Ambedkar.

After twenty years in India, he returned to England to establish the Friends of the Western Buddhist Order (FWBO) in 1967, and the Western Buddhist Order (called Trailokya Bauddha Mahasangha in India) in 1968. Since then, he has devoted much of his time to speaking, writing, and travel, and his depth of experience and clarity of thought have been appreciated throughout the world.

Preface

When I was new to Buddhism and looking for ways in which to practise it, I came across the booklet entitled *Mind – Reactive and Creative*. On reading it, I became very excited at the possibilities it opened up. I realized I had an eminently practical tool that I could apply, then and there, to the life I was leading. I didn't need to be able to reach the sublime heights of meditative absorption (a long way from me at the time) or to take up a robe and bowl. I could use it as I was: working in a human rights organization and living in London – with all the demands, preoccupations, and distractions such a life involves.

With this tool I was able to bring awareness to events that had just 'happened', or to situations in which I felt frustrated or overwhelmed. I realized, as if in a revelation, that I had a choice. I could choose to react unthinkingly to what was happening, or I could pause, try to see things differently, and look for a new way to respond.

Over the years I have remembered this basic teaching of Buddhism, so clearly presented as the creative mind in that booklet. I have put it into practice in traffic jams, meetings, confrontations, and on rainy Monday mornings, alone and with others.

Since then, I have read much more of the teachings of Sangharakshita, including the other title in *Buddha Mind: Breaking Through Into Buddhahood*. In this, too, I was struck by the usefulness of the teaching – and its challenge. Do I really believe in my own potential for Buddhahood? What stands in my way? And am I prepared to make the effort to identify and break through those barriers? Along with the challenge, Sangharakshita also encourages us to have faith in the possibility of breaking through – as well as helping us to identify the hindrances.

Sangharakshita has also expressed his own deep commitment to the Buddhist path in poetry. If we lay prose and poetry side by side we get different, though complementary, insights into the Truth towards which they are pointing. In 'I Want to Break Out....' and 'New', part of which is included in this book, we see Sangharakshita the poet engage personally with the teachings of creativity and spiritual transformation contained in the essays.

In much of his teaching and writing, Sangharakshita consistently poses the challenge that I felt when reading those booklets: the challenge to make the practice of Buddhism a living reality that affects every aspect of one's life. His message is that Buddhism, properly and deeply understood, and thoroughly and extensively applied, is revolutionary. It is not just a pleasant theory or pastime; it can, and should, change our lives.

In both 'Breaking Through Into Buddhahood' and 'Mind – Reactive and Creative' the mind is of central importance in making this change. In Milton's words, it is 'its own place, and in itself / Can make a heaven of hell, a hell of heaven'. But if it is our minds that create our worlds, it is also our minds that contain the key to transformation. Sangharakshita, in a reference to Blake's golden string that leads us in at heaven's gate, talks of our minds as being the beginning of that golden string that eventually leads us to Buddhahood.

If we can learn to work with our mind, and not be at the mercy of negative emotions, habitual reactions, and repetitive thoughts, then we have a valuable tool to help us to make breakthroughs in our spiritual practice, including, one day, that most dramatic breakthrough of all – into Buddhahood.

Jnanasiddhi
July 2001

Experiences are preceded by mind, led by mind, and produced by mind. If one speaks or acts with an impure mind, suffering follows even as the cart-wheel follows the hoof of the ox.

Experiences are preceded by mind, led by mind, and produced by mind. If one speaks or acts with a pure mind, happiness follows like a shadow that never departs.

breaking through into
buddhahood

WE USUALLY THINK of the spiritual life in terms of growth, in terms of progress, development, and evolution. Something slow, steady, proceeding by regular continuous steps. And this concept of gradual evolution is a perfectly valid one, and a very good and helpful way of thinking and speaking of the spiritual life. But we can think of the spiritual life and the spiritual experience in another way, in terms of breaking through, and there are certain advantages in thinking of it in this way. If we think in terms of breaking through – or, if you like, of bursting through – it becomes clear that spiritual life consists, in part at least, or from one point of view at least, in an abrupt transition from one level or dimension of experience, or one mode of being, to another. It draws attention to the fact that the spiritual life involves not just effort, but even violence. The idea that the spiritual life involves violence is not a very popular one, but involve violence it does. Not, of course, violence to others, but violence to oneself, or to certain aspects of oneself that constitute obstacles which need to be overcome. We all come up against these obstacles, these very difficult, obstinate aspects of ourselves, which stand in the way of our higher development and evolution. Sometimes they are very intractable indeed, and we find that they cannot be charmed away by any sort of siren song, nor does it seem possible to remove them or dismantle them bit by bit. There they are in all their intractable tangibility, like great rocks and boulders, blocking our path. Sometimes we just have to break through, to burst through, with the help of a sort of charge of spiritual dynamite, regardless of consequences. It cannot always be easy, gradual, or smooth; sometimes it has to be violent and abrupt, even dramatic. We may say that the average spiritual life consists of periods of fairly steady progress, perhaps even apparent stagnation, separated by more or less violent and dramatic breakthroughs. This is the picture, the graph as it were, of the average spiritual life. There is a period of very slow progress followed by a breakthrough to another, higher level, then another period of slow steady progress and then another breakthrough.

So we are concerned here with the aspect of breakthrough, and we are going to discuss it under three main headings, which are not mutually exclusive: (1) what one breaks through, (2) how one breaks through, and (3) when and where one breaks through.

WHAT ONE BREAKS THROUGH

In principle, one has to break through everything that is mundane, everything that is conditioned, that is 'of this world', that is part and parcel of the saṁsāra; everything that represents a segment or a spoke or an aspect of the Wheel of Life. But this statement, though true, is too general. The mundane, the conditioned, the saṁsāra, has so many different aspects, which are like so many thick impenetrable veils – like so many barriers or road blocks, so many great boulders piled high in our path, all of which have to be broken through. I am going to discuss just four of the more important blockages, or important aspects of the conditioned, of the mundane, that have to be broken through if Buddhahood is to be attained. First of all, negative emotions; secondly, psychological conditionings; thirdly, rational thinking; and fourthly, time sense.

Negative emotions

In their primary form, negative emotions are three in number. There is craving, in the sense of neurotic desire, there is hatred, and there is fear. There are also many secondary and tertiary forms, for example anxiety, insecurity, jealousy, self-pity, guilt, remorse, contempt, conceit, envy, depression, pessimism, gloom, alarm, despondency, despair, suspicion, and resentment. I'm not going to say much about them, as preoccupation with negative emotions is itself very likely to generate negative emotion.

All the negative emotions represent leakages or drainings away of emotional energy. When we indulge in negative emotions, whether in their primary, secondary, or tertiary forms, energy – psychical energy, even spiritual energy – is draining away from us in all directions, all the time. Therefore, indulgence in the negative emotions weakens us and this causes us to withdraw into ourselves, to contract. The effect of indulging constantly and persistently in the negative emotions is that we contract into what we may describe as a cold, hard, tight knot of separate selfhood. Unfortunately, we may say that the negative emotions are extremely widespread, practically all-pervasive, and it seems to be the special function of several ubiquitous agencies to intensify these negative emotions as much as possible.

Take, for example, the daily newspapers, many of which specialize in the sensational, the shocking, and the horrible. In this way negative emotions are stimulated. Then there is the advertising industry, a very large, important, and powerful industry, whose special function seems to be to stimulate neurotic craving, to multiply people's wants rather than to meet their needs. Then again, we find that most people we meet are negative rather than positive in their emotional attitudes and responses. So we have to be very careful not to allow ourselves to be influenced by, to be tinged with, this grey emotional state. We have to break through, to burst through, into a positive emotional state of love, of faith and devotion, of compassion and joy, and we should do our best to encourage positive emotions and attitudes in others.

Psychological conditionings

These may he defined as factors which influence, even determine, our mental attitudes and behaviour without our being fully aware of it or perhaps without our being aware of it at all. Suppose, for instance, we are born in England. We naturally grow up speaking the English language. We are educated in an English school, exposed to all the rigours of the English climate. All this will affect or influence our outlook very deeply without our being aware of it. It will result in an English psychological conditioning rather than, say, a French or Chinese psychological conditioning. The natural result will be that we shall look out upon the world as an Englishman and see things from that special point of view. We may be rather surprised when one day we perhaps wake up to the fact that other people in the world see things rather differently.

This is just one example, but psychological conditioning is of very many different kinds. We are psychologically conditioned by our race, by our class, and by the work we do. Just think of it: you do the same kind of work, in many cases, so many hours of the day, days of the week, weeks of the year, years of your life, so that you start seeing things in a special way, from the standpoint of your employment, you profession, your occupation, your vocation. Moreover, we are psychologically conditioned by the social and economic system of which we are a part and by the religion into which we are born or in which we have been brought up. All this goes to show that we are just a mass of psychological conditioning: a class conditioning, plus an economic conditioning, plus a religious conditioning, plus a national conditioning, plus a linguistic conditioning. There is very little, in fact, that is really ours, really our own. There is very little in our lives and experience that is really free and spontaneous, that is really, in a word, us. For the most part, we think, even feel, and certainly act in certain ways, because we have been conditioned to do so. For the most part we are no better than Pavlov's dogs. A bell rings: we react, we respond; and bells are ringing all the time – religious bells, economic bells, social bells, political bells. The bells go on ringing and ringing, and we respond like mad and call this our freedom. We may say that, really and truly, we are machines rather than human beings.

So we have to break through all these conditionings, we have to shatter, to smash, our own mechanicalness, otherwise there is no Buddhahood – not even, in fact, any real spiritual life.

This breaking through the barriers and obstacles of psychological conditioning means a sort of de-identification of ourselves, a sort of dissociation from that part of ourselves which is machine-like. Spiritual people, we may say, will not think of themselves as being English, or working-class, or middle-class, or any class. They won't think of themselves as townspeople if they live in the town, or as country people if they live in the country. The spiritual person won't think of themselves as essentially being a doctor, or a bus driver, or a housewife, and therefore will not think or feel or act out of any such conditioning. He or she will act freely and spontaneously out of the 'depths' of pure, clear awareness. Such a person eventually won't think of himself as being even a human being. If such a person, such a spiritual person – or, one might even say, transcendental person – thinks at all, which is doubtful, they will think of themself as a Buddha, and will act as a Buddha, because he or she will have broken through all psychological conditioning, will have broken through into Buddhahood.

Rational thinking
This kind of breaking through is indeed difficult to imagine. We can well understand the need for breaking through our negative emotions, which are obviously undesirable. We can understand, with a bit of effort, at least theoretically, the need for breaking through psychological conditioning. But though we understand, it is, after all, our rational mind that is understanding, and now our mind is being asked to contemplate, to agree to, its own dissolution. It's terrifying to experience this even as an idea, even as a thought, even as a concept. The rational mind, we know, is an extremely important faculty. It has been

developed over hundreds of thousands of years of evolution, and is the chief instrument of human survival. It is, therefore, natural that it should be valued very highly, but it should not be overvalued. It is invaluable for practical purposes. After all, it was the rational mind that discovered fire, that invented the wheel, that domesticated animals at the dawn of history, that forged tools and implements, that established cities and systems of government, that built roads and bridges. More recently, the rational mind, the rational intelligence, has created the aeroplane and radio and television. It is the rational mind that split the atom, and it is the rational mind that is at present dreaming, if you can speak of it as dreaming, of interplanetary and intergalactic travel. But though the rational mind may achieve all this, and even more that we cannot even imagine, the rational mind cannot know reality. In the Buddha's words, or rather word, reality – truth itself, the absolute, the unconditioned, the ultimate – is *atakkavacara*. *Takka* or *tarka* means rational thinking, rational thought, even logic, and the Buddha says clearly, emphatically, unmistakably, that in order to experience reality, one must go beyond this, one must break through the rational mind, even break down the rational mind, and only then can one break through into Buddhahood.

For most people, this is very difficult to accept. The rational mind has achieved so much. We like to think that with it we can understand Buddhism, the nature of

Enlightenment, and Zen. In the West, very many books have been written by all sorts of people about Zen – all written with the rational mind – whereas Zen is in fact nothing but a gigantic, overwhelming protest against the assumption, the blasphemous assumption even, that the rational mind can know reality. Zen, we may say, most rudely gives the rational mind a violent slap in the face. Usually, people like to think that the rational mind is omnipotent – that it can do everything, know everything. They don't like to be asked to contemplate the weakness of the rational mind, or to be reminded of the power of the non-rational. For this reason they react, sometimes rather strongly, to things that remind them of the non-rational, or that makes them feel the presence – even the pulling, or the pushing – of the non-rational. This is why some people react rather strongly to things like insanity. It is perhaps rather significant that in this country we lock up the insane, or at least put them away – even the quite harmless ones. In India, by contrast, the insane are allowed to roam freely in the streets of the cities and villages. The Indians are not afraid of the insane, and this is because they are not afraid of the non-rational.

Similarly, we tend to be afraid of our violent emotions, which might carry us away out of ourselves, force us to lose control. We tend to like nice, gentle, soft, tame, manageable emotions. We don't like violent emotions; we react rather strongly to drugs, or to surrealist art, or even to people who are a bit different from us. It is rather significant that gypsies are harassed so much by urban district councils and the like. It is because they represent the unharnessable, the unmanageable, the untameable. They all represent for us the power of the non-rational, they all represent the possibility, and also the danger, of breaking through the rational mind.

Time sense

One could say that time is security, that is, insecurity; but perhaps this is too cryptic. There are two kinds of time – some people say three or four, but let us say two today: organic time and mechanical or clock time. By organic time we mean our own total experience of pure continuous duration, with no thought of before or after, just a direct immediate present. Here there is no splitting up of the time flow into past, present, and future. Mechanical or clock time is the experience of travelling as though along a straight line. This is also sometimes called linear time. It is divided into past, present, and future; it is chopped up into hours, minutes, seconds. Organic time, we may say, expands and contracts, according to the intensity of one's experience. If one's experience is more intense, then organic time expands; if it is less intense, one's organic time contracts. But clock time is relatively uniform, it is the same all the time. So clock time does not correspond to organic time and cannot measure organic time, or one's experience within clock time. When one speaks of breaking through the time sense, or breaking through time, one means mechanical time or clock time.

Most of us, sad to say, especially those of us who live in cities, are slaves of clock time. We live our lives according to the clock. For example, at one o'clock, we say it is time to eat, whether or not we feel hungry. In the same way we work when it is time to work, sleep when it is time to sleep, and even meditate when it is time to meditate – often for no other reason. Our lives are geared to the clock, and in this way the natural self-regulating rhythm of the organism is disrupted, and one's experience of organic time, of pure duration, is lost. Our life's experiences don't emerge and flower from the depths of the eternal now. We see them strung out, like washing on a line, and therefore we mentally anticipate our experiences, we mentally pre-arrange them. We draw up programmes and diaries and so on because, basically, we don't trust ourselves to the experience of organic time, of pure continuous duration – we feel insecure. (This is why I said that time is security, and therefore insecurity.) We like to think within this context of clock time, 'Well, tomorrow is Monday, I'll be doing such-and-such; next week I'll be doing this, next year I'll be doing that.' So some people plan and organize their whole lives in this way, right up to the day of retirement, and after that, of course, there is just a blank, a sort of dreary miserable space before death, and this is a really frightening thought. I suppose it is not altogether our own individual fault, because pressure is brought upon us all the time to live in this way, to regulate our lives and gear our existence to the clock – which of course means not really living at all. So we have to break through the time sense, break through mechanical time. We have, as it were, to smash the clock, or at least allow it to run down.

A Vision of Freedom

So we must break through negative emotions, through psychological conditioning, through rational thinking, and through the time sense. In this way, from all these four angles and directions simultaneously, we can break through into, or converge upon, Buddhahood.

Now Buddhahood has various aspects which correspond to different aspects of the conditioned, the mundane, the saṁsāra. If we break through the conditioned at a certain point, we shall break through into the corresponding aspect of Buddhahood. If, for instance, we break through the suffering of conditioned existence, we shall break through into the bliss, the happiness, the everlasting joy, of Buddhahood. Similarly with regard to the four aspects of the conditioned with which we have been dealing. Breaking through the negative emotions means breaking through into the positive emotions of love and compassion. Breaking through psychological conditioning means breaking through into a state of complete freedom, spontaneity, and unconditioned creativity. Breaking through the rational mind means breaking through into a state of what we may describe as transcendental non-rationality. Finally, breaking through the time sense means breaking through into the experience of the eternal everlasting now.

What would a Buddha be like?

Love and compassion, freedom and spontaneity, transcendental non-rationality, and living in the eternal now are all aspects of Buddhahood, and are also characteristics of the enlightened person. The enlightened person will manifest, will radiate, positive emotions, will be completely unconditioned and spontaneous in behaviour and will therefore be unpredictable. He may be liable to do anything at any moment, will not be bound by rational thinking, and will be quite devoid of any sense of mechanical time, living from moment to moment and enjoying, as it were, the bliss of pure duration. From all this we can see that the enlightened person cuts a rather unconventional figure.

Some Hindu texts raise the question: How would the liberated, enlightened person appear to others? Within himself he would know reality, would know God or Brahman, but what would he look like to others? Some of the texts give a threefold reply. They say that the enlightened person will appear like a child, like a madman, and like a ghost. Like a child because the child is spontaneous and uninhibited, like a madman because the enlightened person in a sense is just mad, and like a ghost because the ghost just comes and goes, you don't know where from or where to. The enlightened person is like that. You cannot tie him down or corner him. You cannot keep track of him: he slips through your fingers. There is also something a little uncanny about him. The enlightened person, one may say, will certainly not appear to other people like a respectable and law-abiding citizen.

HOW ONE BREAKS THROUGH

The way of mindfulness

Breaking through any aspect of conditioned existence, any aspect of the Wheel of Life, is accomplished mainly through the cultivation of awareness, mindfulness, and recollection. Awareness, we may say, is the great dissolver of negative emotions, of psychological conditionings, in fact every aspect of the conditioned within ourselves. There is no spiritual life without awareness. An action, thought, or feeling is spiritual to the extent that it is accompanied by awareness. If there is anything negative in the thought, feeling, or action, anything that smacks of the conditioned, then the awareness with which it is done, if that awareness is maintained, will sooner or later eat away at all the conditioning and negativity, So awareness is of paramount importance in the spiritual life. There is no spiritual life, no breakthrough, without awareness.

A path of regular steps

Breaking through is also accompanied by means of regular spiritual practice of one kind or another: puja, making offerings, meditation, giving dana. Every time one practises, an effect is produced. The practice may be very little, very limited, but there is an effect. If you keep up the limited practice, and if it is regular – daily, even hourly – then the effect accumulates within the form of what the Yogacara calls the 'good seeds'. If we keep up the regular practice long enough, these 'good seeds' within us, these wholesome effects, will accumulate to the point of bursting and there will be a breakthrough. But of course, if we do things in this way, we must have patience. An example often given is that of the rock which is split by the twentieth blow. The first nineteen were not useless, though they did not appear to have any effect. Without them the twentieth blow could not have done its work. So this is another way of breaking through: keeping up these strokes, i.e. the regular practice, month after month, year after year: ten, twenty, thirty years. The effects accumulate, tensions accumulate, and then one breaks through. Breakthrough is also achieved by the introduction into one's life of a new factor, especially of a new person – something or someone who jolts us out of our accustomed routine, who breaks up our accustomed routine, who gets us to some extent out of our conditioning. How does one break through the four aspects of the conditioned already mentioned?

Breaking through negative emotions

One breaks through negative emotions principally by cultivating the positive emotions. Here, practices like the *mettā bhāvanā*, the development of universal loving kindness, though rather difficult, help very much. One can also break through negative emotions by associating more with people who are emotionally positive, who are either full of love and compassion, of joy and confidence, or even just ordinary cheerfulness. Also, eating the right kind of food can help – not the kind that clogs the system and weighs you down, making you feel heavy and stiff and lethargic. One can also break through into the positive emotions, to some extent, by living more in the open air, by staying in the sunshine as much as possible, looking at green grass and blue sky, and by surrounding oneself with bright colours. Perhaps one should dress more brightly, more colourfully, because this too has a positive emotional effect.

Breaking through psychological conditionings

One breaks through psychological conditionings mainly, of course, through awareness: awareness that one is conditioned, is mechanical, is not free. But how does one develop this sort of awareness? How does one extend and amplify it? One can sometimes do this by subjecting oneself, quite deliberately, to an unfamiliar type of conditioning. If, for instance, one's psychological conditioning is English, then one could go and live for a time in Italy, or India, or Japan. In this way one will become aware of one's own conditioning, because one will have become aware of the unfamiliar conditioning of the people in the midst of whom one is living. Their conditioning will impinge, sometimes rather uncomfortably, on your conditioning. For instance, people in India eat with their fingers. At first English people are often very shocked by this and think it terribly unhygienic. After a time, however, you get used to it, and you realize that it was because of your own conditioning that you were shocked. So to the extent that you become aware of your conditioning, to that extent you become free from it. For this reason it is very good to travel and see new countries, meet new people of different races, religions, colours, and cultures. As we get older – and we're getting older every day – the general tendency is to visit only the old familiar places. We say, 'Ah well, I'll go back there. I went there ten years ago, fifteen years ago. I have been there maybe every year for ten, fifteen, twenty years. Let's have another holiday there. It's the same old hotel keeper, the same old beach; it hasn't changed a bit.' In this way we travel in the same old rut over and over again.

Breaking through rational thinking

This is something rather more difficult to do. Traditionally there are several ways. The Perfection of Wisdom literature employs the method of paradox. A paradox has been defined or described as a truth standing on its head to attract attention, but it's really much more than that. The paradox is a using of conceptual thought to transcend conceptual thought. In the Perfection of Wisdom texts, for instance, the Buddha says that the Bodhisattva, the one who wants to gain Enlightenment for the sake of all, must vow to save all beings. He must vow, 'I'll deliver, I'll save, I'll help all beings in the universe.' And then, the Buddha goes on to say, he must at the same time realize that no beings exist, otherwise he is not a Bodhisattva. In the same way, the texts say that the Bodhisattva must go all out for Enlightenment, practise the perfections, the paramitas, sacrifice life and limb, shed his blood; at the same time he must realize that there is no such thing as Enlightenment, and no one attains it. This is the paradoxical approach to the Perfection of Wisdom literature, which really brings the intellect right up against it.

This sort of method or approach is exemplified, is crystallized, in the koan of Zen. I am not going to try to define a koan, but those of you who have studied the literature on Zen – admittedly literature written mainly with the rational mind – know that the koan is very much used in Zen, especially in the Rinzai School, and that it is a sort of apparently contradictory, or even nonsensical, statement. For instance, when you clap your two hands together, you produce a clapping sound, so the koan says 'What is the sound of one hand clapping?' Or the master says to the disciple, 'What are you carrying?' The disciple replies, 'I'm not carrying anything.' And the master says, 'Well, drop it then.'

There are hundreds of such koans, and in the traditional system the disciple sits in the meditation hall, meditating on one or another of them, hour after hour for days and weeks on end. We are told that sometimes he breaks out in a sweat. He doesn't know whether it is snowing or raining, whether it is spring or autumn, day or night. He is just stuck with this koan, which sometimes becomes like a great lump of ice, or like a red-hot iron ball that he has swallowed: he cannot get it up and he cannot get it down. But eventually he breaks through – he bursts through – the rational mind. This method presupposes a great faith in the master and a strong traditional system of discipline, and is therefore rather difficult to transplant to the West.

But there are other ways of breaking through the rational mind, not perhaps so drastic as the koan method, but certainly still effective. We can, for instance, have more recourse to non-conceptual modes of communication. We can have more recourse to things like myths, legends, and symbols, all of which are nowadays coming more and more into their own. Formerly when people translated the Buddhist scriptures they just cut out all the 'mythical bits', saying that the monks had inserted those much later, and that only the rational bits were the real bits and what the Buddha had actually said. Fortunately for us, Jung has rather altered all that, and has taught us to appreciate and to evaluate these things rather differently. So we have put all the mythological bits back and when we read them we find that they speak to us, that they have a meaning – though not a conceptual meaning. They have a message, they have an impact. There is something that carries over from them above and beyond, or even round about and underneath, the rational mind. These myths, these symbols – whether the ladder down which the Buddha came from heaven to earth, or his seven steps, or his encounter with the earth goddess under the bodhi tree, or Mucalinda – all help to communicate the non-conceptual, trans-conceptual truth of Buddhism, of the Buddha's Enlightenment. So we shouldn't think that communication is only conceptual, only verbal, only a matter of ideas and thoughts and philosophies. We must try to emphasize the importance of the non-conceptual, the mythical, the symbolical – if you like, of the archetypal, the direct, the experiential.

Breaking through the time sense

We can make a very good beginning by doing without a watch. One can also, to some extent, break through mechanical time by having a job which does not oblige one to live according to the clock, where one will not have regular hours, if that is possible. This, I appreciate, is rather difficult to do, except of course for people like artists who can work, we are told, just when they feel like it, without having to stick to any deadline or programme or to keep their eye on the clock.

WHERE AND WHEN ONE BREAKS THROUGH
One may say that the most favourable conditions for breaking through are the unfavourable ones. Usually one does not break through when things are going well, when it is all plain sailing, when everything is going according to plan, One is more likely to break through in times of crisis. The Buddha sweated and struggled and starved himself for six years, and he seemed, to himself at least, to be no nearer his goal. So, according to legend, he sat down under the bodhi tree, and clenched his teeth, and said, 'Flesh may wither away, blood may dry up, but until I have gained Enlightenment I am not getting up from this seat.' So for him it was Enlightenment or death. This was the crisis for him, the crisis which, in a sense, he created for himself.

Some people have been known to break through at a time of physical deprivation. It is as though the weakening of the body strengthens the spirit. Some people have been known to break through when undergoing a prolonged fast. Sometimes, strange to say, one can break through when one is ill. This would seem to be a very unfavourable time: you cannot meditate, sometimes you cannot read; but many people have had important breakthroughs, in fact crucial breakthroughs, at such times. For instance, when you get a high fever – especially in the East this is the case – though you have got the fever, though in a sense you are sick, even suffering, you are sort of strangely exhilarated, and awareness can be intensified, and you can have a breakthrough at that time. You can also have a breakthrough when you have had a shock of some kind: when you have suffered a great bereavement; or when you have lost an enormous sum of money: or your plans have been laid in ruins; or everything has gone hopelessly astray, contrary to your expectations; when you seem to have no hope and no prospects: sometimes in conditions like this you will have a breakthrough.

Death – the crucial situation

According to *The Tibetan Book of the Dead*, one can break through even at the time of death. Death, in a sense, is the greatest crisis, the most crucial situation of all – it also therefore represents the greatest opportunity. According to the tradition which is embodied in *The Tibetan Book of the Dead*, at the time of death, and just after death, one experiences, at least momentarily, what is known as the Clear Light of the Void, the light of Reality shining, as it were, upon one. Transcendental though it is, awe-inspiring though it is, this is not anything that comes from outside: it is the light, the great white light, of one's own true mind, which is identical, ultimately, in its absolute depths, with Reality itself. If one can only recognize this, at that moment, either during the time of death, or just after death, then one is liberated, and there may be for one no more rebirth.

Freedom is frightening

In these pages we have tried to understand what we break through, how we break through, and when and where we break through. Inevitably our approach has been rather conceptual, even though, at the same time, the limitations of the conceptual have been indicated. I would like to end with a picture of breaking through – a picture from Tibetan Buddhism, from the Tantric tradition. It is a picture, an image, a form, of what is known as a wrathful deity or even a wrathful Buddha. What does this wrathful figure look like? How does he appear? First of all, he is a dark blue male figure, very very powerfully built, with a massive torso, enormous legs, and enormous arms. Sometimes naked, sometimes draped in tiger skin, he wears a garland of human skulls. He has a third eye in the middle of his forehead. All three eyes glare with an expression of terrible, terrific anger. From the mouth there stick out fangs and a red blood-dripping tongue. This fearful dark blue figure tramples on enemies – upon ignorance, upon craving – and his hands – sometimes two, sometimes four, sometimes eight, sometimes sixteen, sometimes thirty-two – grasp various weapons. What does this figure, this form, represent? This is the image of breaking through. This fearful, or this wrathful, or this terrific form, represents the forces of Enlightenment breaking, even bursting, through the thick dense darkness of ignorance and unawareness. This form, this image, represents transcendental consciousness at the point of, at the moment

29

VAJRAPANI

of, breaking through into Buddhahood. The whole figure is surrounded by an aureole of flames. And what does the aureole of flames represent? Breaking through on any level, with regard to any medium, entails friction, just as, when a spacecraft re-enters the Earth's atmosphere, there is tremendous friction. Friction generates heat, and heat, when it reaches a certain point, a certain pitch of intensity, results in a conflagration, in a bursting into flames.

So the wrathful Buddha bursting through the conditioned is therefore surrounded by this aureole of flames, and these flames consume and burn up the darkness, burn up everything conditioned. And when everything conditioned is burned up, is consumed, is broken through, then breaking through into Buddhahood is complete, is accomplished. Then there is no more darkness, no more friction, no more flames, but only the shining figure of the Buddha, a Buddha, *another* Buddha, seated beneath the bodhi tree.

I want to break out,
Batter down the door,
Go tramping black heather all day
On the windy moor,
And at night, in hayloft, or under hedge, find
A companion suited to my mind.

I want to break through,
Shatter time and space,
Cut up the Void with a knife,
Pitch the stars from their place,
Nor shrink back when, lidded with darkness, the Eye
Of Reality opens and blinds me, blue as the sky.

'I Want to Break Out ...' by Sangharakshita

mind – reactive and creative

TAKING A BIRD'S-EYE VIEW of human culture, we see
that there exist in the world numerous spiritual traditions. Some of these are of great antiquity, coming down
from the remote past with all the authority and prestige
of that which has been long established; others are of
more recent origin. While some have crystallized, in the
course of centuries, into religious cults with enormous
followings, others have remained more of the nature of
philosophies, making few concessions to popular tastes
and needs. Each one of these traditions has its own
system, that is to say, its own special concatenation – its
own network – of ideas and ideals, of beliefs and practices, as well as its own particular starting-point in
thought or experience out of which the whole system
evolves. This starting-point is the 'golden string' which,
when wound into the ball of the total system, will lead
one in at 'heaven's gate, built in Jerusalem's wall' of the
tradition concerned.

Among the spiritual traditions of the world one of the
oldest and most important is that known to us as

Buddhism, the tradition deriving from the life and teaching of Gautama the Buddha, an Indian master the vibrations of whose extraordinary spiritual dynamism not only electrified north-eastern India in the sixth century BCE but subsequently propagated themselves all over Asia and beyond. Like other traditions Buddhism possesses its own special system and its own distinctive starting point. The system of Buddhism is what is known as the 'Dharma', a Sanskrit word meaning, in this context, the 'Doctrine' or the 'Teaching', and connoting the sum total of the insights and experiences conducive to the attainment of Enlightenment or Buddhahood. Its starting-point is the mind.

A SHARED TRADITION

That this, and no other, is the starting-point, is illustrated by two quotations from what are sometimes regarded as the two most highly antithetical, not to say mutually exclusive, developments within the whole field of Buddhism: Theravada and Zen. According to the first two verses of the *Dhammapada*, an ancient collection of metrical aphorisms included in the Pali Canon of the Theravadins,

> Experiences are preceded by mind, led by mind, and produced by mind. If one speaks or acts with an impure mind, suffering follows even as the cart-wheel follows the hoof of the ox. Experiences are preceded by mind, led by mind, and produced by mind. If one speaks or

acts with a pure mind, happiness follows like a shadow
that never departs.

The Zen quotation is if anything more emphatic. In a
verse which made its appearance in China during the
T'ang dynasty, Zen itself, which claims to convey from
generation to generation of disciples the very heart of
the Buddha's spiritual experience, is briefly characterized as:

> A special transmission outside the Scriptures.
> No dependence on words and letters.
> Direct pointing to the mind.
> Seeing into one's own nature and realizing
>   Buddhahood.

From these quotations, representative of many others
which could be made, it is clear that the starting-point
of Buddhism is not anything outside us. In the language
of Western thought, it is not objective but subjective.
The starting-point is the mind.

ABSOLUTE MIND

But what do we mean by mind? In the *Dhammapada*
verses the original Pali word is *mano*; in the Chinese Zen
stanza it is *hsin*, corresponding to the Sanskrit and Pali
citta. As both these terms can be quite adequately rendered by the English 'mind' there is no need to explore
etymologies and we can plunge at once into the heart
of our subject.

To begin with, mind is twofold. On the one hand there is Absolute Mind; on the other, relative mind. By Absolute Mind is meant that infinite cosmic or transcendental Awareness within whose pure timeless flow the subject–object polarity as we ordinarily experience it is for ever dissolved. For mind in this exalted sense Buddhism employs, according to context, a number of expressions, each with its own distinctive shade of meaning. Prominent among these expressions are the One Mind, the Unconditioned, Buddha-nature, the Void. In the more neutral language of philosophy, Absolute Mind is Reality. It is the realization of Absolute Mind through the dissolution of the subject–object polarity – the waking up to Reality out of the dream of mundane existence – which constitutes Enlightenment, the attainment of Enlightenment being, of course, the ultimate aim of Buddhism.

MIND REACTIVE, MIND CREATIVE

By relative mind is meant the individual mind or consciousness, functioning within the framework of the subject–object polarity, and it is with this mind that we are now concerned. Like mind in general, relative mind or consciousness is of two kinds: reactive and creative. While these are not traditional Buddhist expressions, neither of them rendering any one technical term in any of the canonical languages, they seem to express very well the import of the Buddha's teaching. In any case, the distinction which they represent is of fundamental importance not only in the 'system' of Buddhism but in the spiritual life generally and even in the entire scheme of human evolution. The transition from 'reactive' to 'creative' marks, indeed, the beginning of spiritual life. It is conversion in the true sense of the term. What, then, do we mean by speaking of 'reactive mind' and 'creative mind'?

In the first place, we should not imagine that there are literally two relative minds, one reactive, the other creative. Rather should we understand that there are two ways in which relative mind or the individual consciousness is capable of functioning. It is capable of functioning reactively and it is capable of functioning creatively. When it functions in a reactive manner, it is known as the reactive mind; when it functions in a creative manner, it is known as the creative mind. But there is only one relative mind.

REACTIVE MIND
By the reactive mind is meant our ordinary, everyday mind, the mind that most people use most of the time, or, rather, it is the mind that uses them. In extreme cases, indeed, the reactive mind functions all the time, the creative mind remaining in complete abeyance. People of this type are born, live, and die animals; though possessing the human form they are in fact not human beings at all. Rather than attempt an abstract definition of the reactive mind let us try to grasp its nature by examining some of its actual characteristics.

Reactive mind

In the first place, the reactive mind is a *re*-active mind. It does not really act, but only *re*-acts. Instead of acting spontaneously, out of its own inner fullness and abundance, it requires an external stimulus to set it in motion. This stimulus usually comes through the five senses. We are walking along the street; an advertisement catches our eye, its bright colours and bold lettering making an instant appeal. Perhaps it is an advertisement for a certain brand of cigarette, or for a certain make of car, or for summer holidays on the sun-drenched beaches of some distant pleasure resort. Whatever the goods or services depicted, our attention is attracted, arrested. We go and do what the advertisement is designed to make us do, or make a mental note to do it, or are left with an unconscious disposition to do it as and when circumstances permit. We have not acted, but have been activated. We have *re*-acted.

The reactive mind is, therefore, the conditioned mind. It is conditioned by its object (e.g. the advertisement) in the sense of being not merely dependent upon it but actually determined by it. The reactive mind is not free.

Mechanical mind

Since it is conditioned the reactive mind is, moreover, purely mechanical. As such it can be appropriately described as the 'penny-in-the-slot' mind. Insert the coin, and out comes the packet. In much the same way, let the reactive mind be confronted with a certain situation or experience and it will react automatically, in an entirely mechanical, hence predictable, fashion. Not only our behaviour but even much of our 'thinking' conforms to this pattern. Whether in the field of politics, or literature, or religion, or whether in the affairs of everyday life, the opinions we so firmly hold and so confidently profess are very rarely the outcome of conscious reflection, of our individual effort to arrive at the truth. Our ideas are hardly ever our own. Only too often have they been fed into us from external sources, from books, newspapers, and conversations, and we have accepted them, or rather received them, in a passive and unreflecting manner. When the appropriate stimulus occurs we automatically reproduce whatever has been fed into our system, and it is this purely mechanical reaction that passes for expression of opinion. Truly original thought on any subject is, indeed, extremely rare, though 'original' does not necessarily mean 'different', but rather whatever one creates out of one's own inner resources regardless of whether or not this coincides with something previously created by somebody else. Some, of course, *try* to be different. This can, however, be a subtle form of conditionedness, for in trying to be different such people are still being determined by an object, by whatever or whoever it is they are trying to be different from. They are still *re*-acting, instead of really acting.

Repetitive mind

Besides being conditioned and mechanical, the reactive mind is repetitive. Being 'programmed' as it were by needs of which it is largely unconscious, it reacts to the same stimuli in much the same way, and like a machine therefore goes on performing the same operation over and over again. It is owing to this characteristic of the reactive mind that 'human' life as a whole becomes so much a matter of fixed and settled habit, in a world of routine. As we grow older, especially, we develop a passive resistance to change, preferring to deepen the old ruts rather than strike out in a new direction. Even our religious life, if we are not careful, can become incorporated into the routine, can become part of the pattern, part of the machinery of existence. The Sunday service or the mid-week meditation become fixed as reference points in our lives, buoys charting a way through the dangerous waters of freedom, along with the weekly visit to the cinema and the launderette, the annual holiday at the seaside, and the seasonal spree.

Unaware mind

Above all, however, the reactive mind is the unaware mind. Whatever it does, it does without any real knowledge of what it is doing. Metaphorically speaking, the reactive mind is asleep. Those in whom it predominates can, therefore, be described as asleep rather than awake. In a state of sleep they live out their lives; in a state of sleep they eat, drink, talk, work, play, vote, make love;

in a state of sleep, even, they read books on Buddhism and try to meditate. Like somnambulists who walk with eyes wide open, they only appear to be awake. Some people, indeed, are so fast asleep that for all their apparent activity they can more adequately be described as dead. Their movements are those of a zombie, or a robot with all its controls switched on, rather than those of a truly aware human being. It is with this realization – when we become aware of our own unawareness, when we wake up to the fact that we are asleep – that spiritual life begins. One might, indeed, go so far as to say that it marks the beginning of truly human existence, though this would imply, indeed, a far higher conception of human existence than the word usually conveys – a conception nearer what is usually termed spiritual. This brings us to the second kind of relative mind, to what we have termed the creative mind.

CREATIVE MIND

The characteristics of the creative mind are the opposite of those of the reactive mind. The creative mind does not *re*-act. It is not dependent on, or determined by, the stimuli with which it comes into contact. On the contrary, it is active on its own account, functioning spontaneously, out of the depths of its own intrinsic nature. Even when initially prompted by something external to itself it quickly transcends its original point of departure and starts functioning independently. The creative mind can therefore be said to *respond* rather than to

43

react. Indeed, it is capable of transcending conditions altogether. Hence it can also be said that whereas the reactive mind is essentially pessimistic, being confined to what is given in immediate experience, the creative mind is profoundly and radically optimistic. Its optimism is not, however, the superficial optimism of the streets, no mere unthinking reaction to, or rationalization of, pleasurable stimuli. By virtue of the very nature of the creative mind such a reaction would be impossible. On the contrary, the optimism of the creative mind persists despite unpleasant stimuli, despite conditions unfavourable for optimism, or even when there are no conditions for it at all. The creative mind loves where there is no reason to love, is happy where there is no reason for happiness, creates where there is no possibility of creativity, and in this way 'builds a heaven in hell's despair'.

Independent mind

Not being dependent on any object, the creative mind is essentially non-conditioned. It is independent by nature, and functions, therefore, in a perfectly spontaneous manner. When functioning on the highest possible level, at its highest pitch of intensity, the creative mind is identical with the Unconditioned; that is to say, it coincides with Absolute Mind. Being non-conditioned the creative mind is free; indeed, it is Freedom itself. It is also original in the true sense of the term, being characterized by ceaseless productivity. This productivity is not necessarily artistic, literary, or musical, even though the painting, the poem, and the symphony are admittedly among its most typical, even as among its most strikingly adequate, manifestations. Moreover, just as the creative mind does not necessarily find expression in 'works of art', so what are conventionally regarded as 'works of art' are not necessarily all expressions of the creative mind. Imitative and lacking true originality, some of them are more likely to be the mechanical products of the reactive mind.

Responsive mind

Outside the sphere of the fine arts the creative mind finds expression in productive personal relations, as when through our own emotional positivity others become more emotionally positive, or as when through the intensity of their mutual awareness two or more people reach out towards, and together experience, a dimension of being greater and more inclusive than their separate individualities. In these and similar cases the creative mind is productive in the sense of contributing to the increase, in the world, of the sum total of positive emotion, of higher states of being and consciousness.

Aware mind

Finally, as just indicated the creative mind is above all the aware mind. Being aware, or rather, being Awareness itself, the creative mind is also intensely and radiantly alive. The creative person, as one in whom the creative mind manifests may be termed, is not only more aware than the reactive person but possessed of far greater vitality. This vitality is not just animal high spirits or emotional exuberance, much less still mere intellectual energy or the compulsive urgency of egoistic volition. Were such expressions permissible, one might say it is the Spirit of Life itself rising like a fountain from the infinite depths of existence, and vivifying, through the creative person, all with whom it comes into contact.

SYMBOLS OF MIND

One picture being worth a thousand words, the reactive mind and the creative mind are illustrated by two important Buddhist symbols. These are the symbols of the Wheel of Life and the Path (or Way), otherwise known – more abstractly and geometrically – as the Circle and the Spiral.

The Wheel of Life

The Wheel of Life, or Wheel of Becoming, occupies an important place in Tibetan popular religious art, being depicted in gigantic size on the walls of temples, usually in the vestibule, as well as on a reduced scale in painted scrolls. It consists of four concentric circles.

THE WHEEL OF LIFE

The three poisons
In the first circle, or hub of the Wheel, are depicted a cock, a snake, and a pig, each biting the tail of the one in front. These three animals represent the three 'unskilful roots' or 'poisons' of craving, aversion, and delusion, which are, of course, the three mainsprings of the reactive mind, the first and second being the two principal negative emotions and the third the darkness of spiritual unawareness out of which they arise. Their biting one another's tails signifies their interdependence, or the fact that the circle is a vicious circle.

Around and around
The second circle is divided vertically into two segments, a black one on the right-hand side and a white one on the left. In the black segment the figures of naked human beings, chained together, are seen plunging headlong downwards with expressions of anguish and terror. In the white segment modestly clad figures, carrying *mani*-cylinders (what in the West are erroneously termed 'prayer-wheels') and religious offerings move gently upwards with serene and happy countenances. These two segments represent two opposite movements or tendencies within the Wheel itself, one centripetal and the other centrifugal. In other words, while the black segment represents a movement in the direction of the hub of the Wheel the white segment represents a movement away from the hub and towards the circumference – towards freedom, ultimately, from

the reactive mind. Though in a sense constituting a stage of the Path, or a section of the Spiral, it is still part of the Wheel inasmuch as regression from it, in the form of a transition from the white to the black segment, is liable to occur at any time. The white segment can therefore be regarded as representing states of consciousness intermediate between the reactive mind and the creative mind from which one can either slide back into the former or rise up into the latter. As the presence of the *mani*-cylinders and the religious offerings suggests, the white segment also represents conventional piety, which being part of the process of the reactive mind is not in itself a sufficient means to Enlightenment and from which, therefore, a reaction to a life of vice and impiety – to the black segment – is always possible.

The six realms
The third circle of the Wheel of Life is divided as though by spokes into five or six segments. These are the five or six 'spheres', or planes, of conditioned existence into which sentient beings are reborn in accordance with their skilful and unskilful bodily, verbal, and mental actions, in other words, as the result of their past 'good' and 'bad' karma. These spheres, depicted in Tibetan religious art with great richness of detail, are (proceeding clockwise from the top) those of the gods, the titans, the hungry ghosts, beings in hell, animals, and men. The total number of segments is either five or six depending on whether the gods and the titans, who are

engaged in perpetual warfare with each other, are enumerated separately or together. In all the segments the presence of a differently coloured Buddha figure represents the persistence of the possibility of Enlightenment even under the most adverse conditions.

Although the five or six spheres of conditioned existence are usually interpreted cosmologically – as objectively existing worlds which are just as real, for the beings inhabiting them, as our own world is for human beings – it is nevertheless also possible to interpret them psychologically, as representing different states of human life and consciousness – an interpretation which has some sanction in tradition. Looked at in this way the sphere of the gods represents a life of security and contentment, that of the titans one of jealousy, competition, and aggressiveness, that of the hungry ghosts one of neurotic dependence and craving, that of the beings in hell one of physical and mental suffering, that of the animals one of barbarism and ignorance, while the human sphere represents a mixed state of existence with neither pleasure nor pain predominating. In the course of a single lifetime one may experience all six states, living now as it were in 'heaven', now as it were in 'hell', and so on.

'This being, that becomes'

The fourth and last circle, or rim of the Wheel, is divided into twelve segments, each containing a picture. The twelve pictures (again proceeding clockwise) depict a blind man with a stick, a potter with a wheel and pots, a monkey climbing a flowering tree, a ship with four passengers, one of whom is steering, an empty house, a man and woman embracing, a man with an arrow in his eye, a woman offering a drink to a seated man, a man gathering fruit from a tree, a pregnant woman, a woman in childbirth, and a man carrying a corpse to the cremation-ground. These pictures illustrate the twelve 'links' in the chain of cyclical conditionality, each of which arises in dependence on, or is conditioned by, the one immediately preceding.

- In dependence upon ignorance, the 'first' link of the chain, arise

- the volitional factors which determine the nature of the next rebirth.

- These give rise to consciousness, in the sense of the karmically neutral 'resultant' consciousness, which begins functioning at the moment of conception.

- In dependence on consciousness arises the psychophysical organism.

- In dependence on the psychophysical organism arise the six sense-organs (mind being reckoned as a sixth sense).

- In dependence on these there arises contact with the external world,

- which gives rise to sensation,

- which gives rise to craving,

- which gives rise to grasping,

- which gives rise to 'coming-to-be'.

- In dependence on 'coming-to-be', by which is meant the renewed process of conditioned existence, arises birth, in the sense of rebirth, from which sooner or later there inevitably follows

- death.

As even a bare enumeration of them is sufficient to make clear, the twelve links are primarily regarded as being distributed over three successive lives, the first two belonging to the previous life, the middle eight to the present life, and the last two to the future life. However, just as the five or six spheres of sentient existence can be interpreted psychologically as well as cosmologically, so the whole twelve-linked chain of cyclical conditionality is also to be regarded as operating within the limits of a single experience of the reactive mind.

Completing the symbolism, Tibetan religious art depicts the whole Wheel of Life, with its four circles and its innumerable sentient creatures, as being gripped from behind by a monstrous demon, the head, tail, and claws of whom are visible. This is the demon of Impermanence, or the great principle of Change, which though dreadful to the majority nevertheless contains the promise and potentiality of development, of evolution.

The wheel as symbol

From the description just given it is clear that the Tibetan Wheel of Life is able to symbolize the workings of the reactive mind because the reactive mind is itself a wheel. Like a wheel, it simply goes round and round. Prompted by negative emotions springing from the depths of unawareness, it again and again reacts to stimuli impinging on it from the outside world, and again and again precipitates itself into one or another sphere or mode of conditioned existence. Moreover, the wheel is a machine, perhaps the most primitive of all machines, and as such the Wheel of Life represents the mechanical and repetitive nature of the reactive mind.

Some paintings of the Wheel of Life depict in their top right-hand corner the Buddha, clad in the saffron robes of a wanderer, pointing with the fingers of his right hand. He is indicating the Path or Way. To this symbol, second of the two great symbols with which we are concerned, we must now turn.

THE SPIRAL PATH

As previously explained, just as the Wheel of Life symbolizes the reactive mind, so the Path or Way symbolizes the creative mind, or the whole process of cumulative, as distinct from reactive, conditionality. It works on the principle not of *round and round*, but of *up and up*. In the case of the Wheel of Life, as depicted in Tibetan religious art, practically all the different aspects of the reactive mind coalesce into a single composite symbol of marvellous richness and complexity. For the Path or Way there seems to be no corresponding picture. Instead, there are a number of relatively independent representations, some of them in the form of images, others in the form of conceptual formulations of the various successive stages of the Path. Among the former are the images of the Tree of Enlightenment, or Cosmic Tree, at the foot of which the Buddha seated himself on the eve of his great attainment, and the ladder of gold, silver, and crystal on which, after instructing his deceased mother in the higher truths of Buddhism, he descended to earth from the Heaven of the Thirty-three Gods. Among the conceptual formulations of the Path are the Three Trainings (i.e. ethics, meditation, and wisdom), the Noble Eightfold Path, the series of twelve positive 'links' beginning with suffering and ending with knowledge of the destruction of the biases, the Seven Stages of Purification, and the Seven Limbs of Enlightenment. All these concrete images and conceptual formulations of the Path represent one or another aspect of the total process of the creative mind, a process of such multi-faceted splendour that tradition has been unable, apparently, to combine them all into one composite representation of their common object. For the purpose of our present exposition we shall select one of the conceptual formulations of the Path, that of the Seven Limbs of Enlightenment, as this exhibits in a particularly clear and striking manner the cumulative and truly progressive nature of the creative mind.

The seven factors of enlightenment

The seven 'limbs' or 'factors' (*anga*) of Enlightenment (*bodhi*) are: Recollection or Awareness, Investigation of Mental States, Energy or Vigour, Rapture, 'Tension Release', Concentration, and Tranquillity. Each of these limbs or factors arises in dependence on the one immediately preceding – out of its fullness, as it were – and as we shall now see in detail, each one, as it arises, constitutes a still higher development of the creative mind as it spirals towards the final – and everlasting – explosion of creativity that constitutes Enlightenment.

1. Recollection or Awareness (smṛti)

As insisted once already, spiritual life begins with awareness, when one becomes aware that one is unaware, or when one wakes up to the fact that one is asleep. Within the context of the total evolutionary process this 'limb' or 'factor', the emergence of which constitutes one a human being, occupies a middle place, being intermediate between the total unawareness, or unconsciousness, of the stone, and the Perfect Awareness of Buddhahood. Within the comparatively narrow but still aeonic context of purely human development, awareness occupies a middle position between the simple sense consciousness of the animal and the higher

55

spiritual awareness of the person who has begun to confront the transcendental. Thus we arrive at a hierarchy which, excluding unconsciousness and the vegetative sensitivity of the plant, consists of the four principal degrees of (a) sense consciousness, (b) human consciousness or awareness proper, (c) transcendental awareness, and (d) Perfect Awareness. As one of the limbs of Enlightenment or Enlightenment factors, Recollection or Awareness corresponds to the second of these degrees, that of human consciousness or awareness proper. Awareness in this sense is synonymous with self-consciousness, a term which draws attention to one of the most important characteristics of awareness. Whereas sense consciousness is simply consciousness of external things and of one's own experience, awareness consists in being conscious that one is conscious, in knowing that one knows, or, in a word, of *realizing*. Though the traditional vocabulary of Buddhism does not contain any term strictly correspondent with self-consciousness, the explanation which is given makes it clear that this is what, in fact, it is. Awareness consists, according to the texts, of awareness of one's bodily posture and movements, of one's sensations, whether pleasurable or painful, and of the presence within oneself of skilful and unskilful mental states. More will be said about each of these later on.

2. Investigation of Mental States (dharma-vicāya)

From awareness in general we pass to awareness, particularly, of the psychical as distinct from the physical side of our being. This psychical side is not static but dynamic. It is made up of an endless stream of mental states. These states are of two kinds, skilful and unskilful. Unskilful mental states are those rooted in craving, hatred, and delusion. Skilful mental states are those rooted in non-craving, non-hatred, and non-delusion, in other words in contentment, love, and wisdom. Investigation of Mental States is a kind of sorting-out operation whereby one distinguishes between the skilful and the unskilful states and separates them into two different categories. In terms of our present discussion one distinguishes between what in the mind is reactive and what is creative. It is, however, awareness that releases creativity. By becoming more aware we not only resolve unawareness, thus eventually achieving self-consciousness or true individuality, but also effect a switch-over of energy from the cyclical to the spiral type of conditionality, that is to say, from the reactive and repetitive to the free and creative type of mental functioning.

3. Energy or Vigour (vīrya)

Although often defined as the effort to cultivate skilful and eradicate unskilful mental states, the third Enlightenment factor is much more in the nature of a spontaneous upsurge of energy coming about with the birth of awareness and the growing capacity to discriminate between the reactive and the creative mind. Most people live far below the level of their optimum vitality. Their energies are either expended in ways that are ultimately frustrating or simply blocked. With increased awareness, however, through meditation, and through improved communication with other people – perhaps with the help of a freer lifestyle and more truly fulfilling means of livelihood – a change takes place. Blockages are removed, tensions relaxed. More and more energy is released. Eventually, like a great dynamo humming into activity as soon as the current is switched on, or a tree bursting into bloom as the spring rain flushes up through its branches, the whole being is recharged, revitalized, and one expends oneself in intense creative activity.

4. Rapture (prīti)

Release of blocked and frustrated energy is accompanied by an overwhelming feeling of delight and ecstasy which is not confined to the mind but in which the senses and the emotions both participate. This is Rapture, the fourth Enlightenment factor, of which there are five degrees. These five degrees produce physical innervations of corresponding degrees of intensity. The lesser thrill is only able to raise the hairs of the body, momentary rapture is like repeated flashes of lightning, flooding rapture descends on the body like waves breaking on the seashore, in all-pervading rapture the whole body is completely surcharged, blown like a full bladder or like a mountain cavern pouring forth a mighty flood of water, while transporting rapture is so strong that it lifts the body up to the extent of launching it in the air. Under ordinary circumstances only prolonged meditation enables one to experience Rapture in its fullness, from the lowest to the highest degree, but this is not to say that it cannot be experienced to a great extent in other ways as well. The creation and enjoyment of works of art, appreciation of the beauties of nature, solving problems in mathematics, authentic human communication – these and similar activities all involve release of energy and all are, therefore, experienced as intensely pleasurable.

5. *Tension Release (praśrabdhi)*

Blocked and frustrated energy having been fully released, the physical innervations by which the release was accompanied gradually subside and the mind experiences a state of non-hedonic spiritual happiness unmixed with any bodily sensation. Subsidence of the physical innervations of Rapture, as well as of the perceptions and motivations derived therefrom, is known as Tension Release. This Enlightenment factor, the fifth in the series, thus represents the stage of transition from the psychosomatic to the mental-spiritual level of experience. Awareness of one's physical body and one's surroundings becomes minimal, or disappears entirely, and one becomes more and more deeply absorbed in a state of 'changeless, timeless bliss' quite impossible to describe.

6. Concentration (samādhi)

Impelled by the inherent momentum of one's experience, absorption in this state gradually becomes complete. Such total absorption is known as *samādhi*. Though untranslatable by any one English word, this term is usually rendered as concentration, a meaning which it admittedly does bear in many contexts. As the sixth of the Enlightenment factors, *samādhi* stands for very much more than simple fixation of the mind on a single object, especially if this fixation is understood as something that is achieved forcibly, by sheer exercise of will, or despite strong resistance from other parts of the psyche. Rather is it the spontaneous merging of all the energies of the psyche in an experience so intensely pleasurable that thought and volition are suspended, space vanishes, and time stands still. It is in fact a state of total integration and absorption rather than of 'concentration' in the more limited and artificial sense of the term, and as such can be compared best, though still inadequately, to the experience of the musician rapt in the enjoyment of a piece of music or of the lover immersed in the joys of love.

7. Tranquillity (upekṣā)

When perfectly concentrated the mind attains a state of poise and equilibrium free from the slightest trace of wavering or unsteadiness. This equilibrium is not only psychological as between contrary emotional states but spiritual as between such pairs of opposites as enjoyment and suffering, acquisition and deprivation, self and not-self, finite and infinite, existence and non-existence, life and death. As a spiritual state or experience it is known as Tranquillity, the seventh and last of the Enlightenment factors and the culmination, so far as this formulation is concerned, of the whole process of the creative mind. Though sometimes connoting simply a psychological state of security and rest it is here synonymous with Nirvāṇa or Enlightenment itself. It is that state of absolute metaphysical axiality – of complete equilibrium of *being* – to which the Buddha refers in the *Maṅgala Sutta*, or 'Discourse on Auspicious Signs', saying:

> He whose firm mind, untroubled by the touch
> Of all terrestrial happenings whatsoe'er,
> Is void of sorrow, stainless and secure –
> This is the most auspicious sign of all.

THE CRUCIAL POINT

In this manner, each member of the series arising out of the abundance – even the exuberance – of the one by which it was immediately preceded, the seven Enlightenment factors collectively illustrate the way in which the creative mind functions, how it progresses from perfection to ever greater perfection, until the fullness of creativity is attained. But having arrived at this point, thus completing our brief study of the two principal symbols of Buddhism, we cannot help asking what the connection is between them. At what point, if any, do the Wheel and the Path, the Circle and the Spiral, intersect?

In order to answer this question we shall have to refer back to the twelve links in the chain of cyclical conditionality. Besides being distributed over three successive lifetimes, these are regarded as being either volitions or the results of volitions and as belonging, therefore, either to what is known as the cause-process or to what is known as the effect-process. Ignorance and the karma-formations, the first two links, constitute the cause-process of the past. They represent the sum total of karmic factors responsible for the present birth, or rather rebirth, of the individual concerned. Consciousness, the psychophysical organism, the six sense-organs, contact, and feeling make up the effect-process of the present life. Craving, grasping, and coming-to-be are the cause-process of the present life, while birth together with old age, disease, and death constitute the effect-process of the future. From this account it is clear that feeling, the last link of the effect-process of the present life, is immediately followed by craving, the first link of the cause-process of the present life. This is the crucial point. This is the point at which the Wheel either stops, or begins to make a fresh revolution. It is also the point of intersection between the Wheel and the Path.

Mindfulness clear and radiant

As we have seen, the first of the seven Enlightenment factors is Recollection or Awareness. If we remain simply aware of the pleasurable and painful feelings that arise within us as a result of our contact with the external world, instead of reacting to them with craving and aversion, then craving, the first link of the cause-process of the present life, will be unable to come into existence. Awareness puts as it were a brake on the Wheel. For this reason the cultivation of Awareness occupies a central place in the Buddhist scheme of spiritual self-discipline. It is the principal means of transition from the reactive mind to the creative mind, from the Wheel to the Path, from the Circle to the Spiral – ultimately, from Saṁsāra to Nirvāṇa.

Tradition distinguishes four different kinds of awareness, or four different levels on which it is to be cultivated:

- In the first place, one is aware of one's bodily posture and movements. This consists in the awareness that one is, for example, standing, or sitting, or walking, or lying down, as well as in the mindful performance of all bodily actions, from the vigorous use of the morning toothbrush to the delicate wielding, the almost imperceptible manipulation, of the surgeon's scalpel or the artist's brush.

- Secondly, one is aware of one's feelings, pleasant, painful, and neutral, as well as of the emotions arising in direct or indirect dependence upon them. One knows whether one feels elated or depressed, whether one's emotional state is one of love or hatred, hope or fear, frustration or fulfilment, and so on. One is also aware of more complex and ambivalent emotions. In order to be aware of one's feelings and emotional reactions one must of course allow oneself to experience them, one must recognize and acknowledge them as one's own. This is not to recommend emotional self-indulgence, but only to emphasize the fact that repression and awareness are incompatible.

- Thirdly, one is aware of one's thoughts. This consists not only of the vigilant observation of images and ideas, mental associations, trains of reflection, and conceptual systems, but also in seeing to what extent these are rooted in the unskilful states of neurotic craving, aversion, and spiritual ignorance, and to what extent they are rooted in the opposite states, that is to say in states of contentment, love, and wisdom. Practising these three kinds of awareness, or cultivating awareness on these three different levels, we begin to see how conditioned we are, how machine-like in our functioning, how dead.

- Fourthly and lastly, one is aware of the difference between one's past dead state of mental conditionedness and mechanicalness and one's (potential) more alive future state of freedom and spontaneity. Awareness of the Wheel and of the fact that one is bound on the Wheel generates awareness of the Path, as well as of the fact that one has the capacity to follow it.

THE DYNAMIC OF SPIRITUAL GROWTH

Awareness is therefore of crucial importance in human existence. As the bud presages the flower, so the development of awareness heralds the dawn of the still higher development that we term the spiritual life. Such being the case it is not surprising that in Buddhism there are a number of practices designed to promote the growth of this all-important quality, but it must be emphasized that unless we exercise the utmost caution these practices will themselves tend to become mechanical and, therefore, bricks in the prison-house of our conditionedness rather than the implements of its destruction. The same warning applies to all 'religious' beliefs and practices without exception. If eternal vigilance is the price of mundane liberty how much more is it the price of spiritual freedom! Whether studying mystical theology or making votive offerings, engaging in spiritual discussion with friends or reading about 'Mind – Reactive and Creative', unless we remember the Buddha's 'Parable of the Raft' and constantly remind ourselves what the true function of all these activities is, there is the danger that we shall find ourselves not midstream on the Raft, not bound for the Further Shore, but on the contrary taking refuge in a structure which, while apparently constructed out of the same materials as the Raft, nevertheless remains firmly stuck in the mudflats of this shore. Only by remaining constantly on our guard shall we succeed in making the difficult transition from the reactive mind to the creative mind, thus inheriting the spirit of the Buddha's teaching and realizing the true purpose of human life.

I should like to speak
With a new voice, telling
The new things that I know, chanting
In incomparable rhythms
New things to new men, singing
The new horizon, the new vision
The new dawn, the new day.
I should like to use
New words, use
Words pristine, primeval, words
Pure and bright as snow-crystals, words
Resonant, expressive, creative,
Such as, breathed to music, built Ilion.
(The old words
Are too tired soiled stale lifeless.)
New words
Come to me from the stars
From your eyes from
Space
New words vibrant, radiant, able to utter
The new me, able
To build for new
Men a new world.

Extract from 'New' by Sangharakshita

Further Reading

Martine Batchelor, *Principles of Zen*, Thorsons, London 1999

Robin Cooper, *The Evolving Mind*, Windhorse, Birmingham 1996

Francesca Fremantle and Chögyam Trungpa (trans.), *The Tibetan Book of the Dead*, Shambhala, Boulder and London, 2000

Henepola Gunaratana, *Mindfulness in Plain English*, Wisdom Publications, Boston 1992

Kulananda, *The Wheel of Life*, Windhorse, Birmingham 2000

Paramananda, *Change Your Mind*, Windhorse, Birmingham 2000

Sangharakshita (trans.), *Dhammapada*, Windhorse, Birmingham 2001

Subhuti, *The Buddhist Vision*, Windhorse, Birmingham 2001

Shunryu Suzuki, *Zen Mind, Beginner's Mind*, Weatherhill, New York and Tokyo 1999

The Windhorse symbolizes the energy of the enlightened mind carrying the Three Jewels – the Buddha, the Dharma, and the Sangha – to all sentient beings.

Buddhism is one of the fastest-growing spiritual traditions in the Western world. Throughout its 2,500-year history, it has always succeeded in adapting its mode of expression to suit whatever culture it has encountered.

Windhorse Publications aims to continue this tradition as Buddhism comes to the West. Today's Westerners are heirs to the entire Buddhist tradition, free to draw instruction and inspiration from all the many schools and branches. Windhorse publishes works by authors who not only understand the Buddhist tradition but are also familiar with Western culture and the Western mind. Manuscripts welcome.

For orders and catalogues contact

WINDHORSE PUBLICATIONS	WINDHORSE BOOKS	WEATHERHILL INC
11 PARK ROAD	P O BOX 574	41 MONROE TURNPIKE
BIRMINGHAM	NEWTOWN	TRUMBULL
B13 8AB	NSW 2042	CT 06611
UK	AUSTRALIA	USA

Windhorse Publications is an arm of the Friends of the Western Buddhist Order, which has more than sixty centres on five continents. Through these centres, members of the Western Buddhist Order offer regular programmes of events for the general public and for more experienced students. These include meditation classes, public talks, study on Buddhist themes and texts, and 'bodywork' classes such as t'ai chi, yoga, and massage. The FWBO also runs several retreat centres and the Karuna Trust, a fund-raising charity that supports social welfare projects in the slums and villages of India.

Many FWBO centres have residential spiritual communities and ethical businesses associated with them. Arts activities are encouraged too, as is the development of strong bonds of friendship between people who share the same ideals. In this way the FWBO is developing a unique approach to Buddhism, not simply as a set of techniques, less still as an exotic cultural interest, but as a creatively directed way of life for people living in the modern world.

If you would like more information about the FWBO visit the website at www.fwbo.org or write to

LONDON BUDDHIST CENTRE	ARYALOKA
51 ROMAN ROAD	HEARTWOOD CIRCLE
LONDON	NEWMARKET
E2 OHU	NH 03857
UK	USA

ALSO FROM WINDHORSE

TEJANANDA

THE BUDDHIST PATH TO AWAKENING

The word Buddha means 'one who is awake'. In this accessible introduction, Tejananda alerts us to the Buddha's wake-up call, illustrating how the Buddhist path can help us develop a clearer mind and a more compassionate heart.

Drawing on over twenty years of Buddhist meditation and study, Tejananda gives us a straightforward and encouraging description of the path of the Buddha and his followers – the path that leads ultimately to our own 'awakening'.

224 pages, with diagrams
ISBN 1 899579 02 8
£8.99/$17.95

VESSANTARA

TALES OF FREEDOM
WISDOM FROM THE BUDDHIST TRADITION

Stories have the power to transform us as we enter their world. Drawn from the rich variety of the Buddhist tradition, these beautifully-told stories convey a sense of inner freedom. We see ordinary people liberate themselves from anger and grief, and great teachers remain free even in the face of death. Vessantara's commentary shows us how we can move towards that freedom in our own lives.

216 pages
ISBN 1 899579 27 3
£9.99/$19.95